GU00862943

Children with special needs in pre-school
Having regard to the DfEE Code of Practice on the identification
and assessment of special educational needs

Text by Meg Bender and Ann Henderson

Cover design by The Jenkins Group
Typeset & printed by CPL Associates

Children with special needs in pre-school

CONTENTS　　　　　　　　　　　　　　　　Page

Introduction

The Code of Practice on the Identification and Assessment of Special Educational Needs provides a valuable framework for ensuring that children with special educational needs are identified and assessed at an early stage and that they are then properly provided for. It applied originally only to schools in the state sector. However, the Nursery Education and Grant Maintained Schools Act 1996 Section IV requires groups in the voluntary and private sectors which receive public funding for nursery education to have regard to the Code of Practice and this requirement came into effect from April, 1997.

Under the terms of the Education Act 1993, a child has a special educational need if s/he has a learning difficulty which calls for special educational provision to be made for her/him. A child has a learning difficulty if:

- s/he has significantly greater difficulty in learning than the majority of children that age

- s/he has a difficulty which either prevents or hinders her/him from making use of educational facilities of a kind generally provided for children of that age in schools within the area of the local authority

or

- s/he is under the age of five years and is, or would be if educational provision were not made for her/him, likely to fall within the two categories identified above.

Children with special educational needs include those with disabilities and those who have learning, language and behaviour difficulties. It is estimated that approximately 20% of children may have some form of special educational need at some time in their education. For the vast majority of these children their needs will be met in mainstream provision which includes voluntary pre-schools, with outside help if necessary. However, a small minority of children, around 2%, will have such severe and complex special educational needs that special arrangements for their education will be required and this will necessitate a statement of special educational needs.

When the Code of Practice first began to be applied to non-statutory provision, it was recognised that not all the required procedures could be implemented immediately. However, all pre-schools should have a sound knowledge of the requirements of the Code of Practice and should have an agreed action plan which sets out how they plan to implement the Code throughout their practice.

For most pre-schools, implementing the Code of Practice will not involve major adjustments. Many of the Code's requirements reflect the good practice already recommended in the publications of the Pre-school Learning Alliance, in particular:

- Having a clear policy on the admission and support of children with special educational needs

- Working in close partnership with parents

- Providing individual support for children and families by means of the keyworker system

- Keeping records based on each child's needs and progress, which celebrate the child's individual achievements, however small

- Adjusting provision as necessary in the light of observation and record-keeping, establishing an on-going 'cycle of quality'.

Pre-schools which are already working in accordance with these principles will have no difficulty in making the adjustments to their systems which may be required by the Code of Practice. This book aims to provide information and advice about the Code of Practice. It will help pre-schools develop and implement plans to bring within a recognised statutory framework the valuable work they are already doing to support children with special educational needs and their families.

Chapter 1

The Code of practice

The principles behind the Code

The major principles of the Code, and their implications for pre-schools, are:

- The needs of all children who may have special educational needs must be addressed; the code recognises that there is a continuum of need which can be met in a wide variety of different ways in different pre-school settings.

- Children with special educational needs should have full access to a broad and balanced pre-school curriculum leading to the National Curriculum at five years of age.

- Children with special educational needs should, where appropriate, be educated alongside their peers in mainstream provision, which includes voluntary pre-schools and private nurseries. The needs of most children will be met in mainstream provision and   without a formal assessment or a statement of special educational needs.

- All children with special educational needs should be identified and assessed as early and as quickly as possible. This will lead to the early development of an appropriate educational programme. Early intervention aims to avoid the escalation of a difficulty into a more serious special educational need.

- Children under five may have special educational needs requiring the assistance of outside professional agencies such as an educational psychologist or the health services.

- The knowledge, views and experience of parents are vital. Effective assessment and appropriate provision are possible only where there are positive partnerships between parents, children and pre-school.

- Wherever possible the views of the child should be considered.

- There must be good co-operation between the pre-school, parents and any outside agencies, in order to provide a genuine, multi-disciplinary approach.

- Few children arrive at pre-school with a statement of special educational need. Most children in need of special support will be identified whilst attending the pre-school but will not need a formal statement of special educational needs.

Implications for practice in pre-school

It is the responsibility of the management committee/owner in a community pre-school/private nursery to ensure that appropriate provision is made for children with special educational needs. Committees and owners will, of course, delegate day-to-day responsibility to the pre-school leader and staff, but they must ensure that the policies and procedures are set up, implemented and reviewed.

Many pre-schools and nurseries, particularly groups accredited by the Pre-school Learning Alliance, already operate according to the policies and guidelines which are promoted by the Pre-school Learning Alliance and will therefore be working within the spirit of the Code of Practice. They will already be providing appropriately for a child or children with special educational needs who will benefit from pre-school education alongside other children. Such pre-schools will already have:

- a special educational needs policy

- a high staff:child ratio

- premises which have been evaluated in the light of the group's commitment to meeting children's special needs

- an appropriate pre-school curriculum

- a development plan

- a commitment to working in partnership with parents

- practice in working in partnership with outside agencies.

- policies on confidentiality.

Special educational needs policy

The committee or owner together with the pre-school leader, other members of staff and parents will be involved in discussing, agreeing and documenting the policy. It is important that the full adult team agrees with and supports the policy and is committed to implementing it. It is important too that parents are fully informed, consulted and involved in the annual review of the policy. In a charitable group this may take place at the AGM. The policy should include the following:

- the objectives of the pre-school's special educational needs policy, to emphasise that the pre-school wishes to provide inclusive experiences for all children, including those with special educational needs

- the policy and arrangements for the admission and integration of children which ensure equal opportunities for children with special educational needs

- arrangements for fostering positive partnerships with parents in all aspects of special educational needs work

- the name of the designated member of staff who has special responsibility for special educational needs within his/her job description (the special educational needs co-ordinator)1

- the arrangements for an appropriate record system for special educational needs work

- the arrangements for the identification and assessment of children

- how children with special educational needs are to be provided with a broad and balanced pre-school curriculum

- information about the resources within the annual budget to be allocated to children with special educational needs

- arrangements for considering complaints about special educational provision

- plans for the in-service training of staff, parents and committee members about special educational needs work

- links with health and social services, the local education authority and other voluntary organisations such as Portage, and how the pre-school will access external support services

- arrangements for reviewing the special educational needs policy and procedures.

Staff:child ratios

The 1989 Children Act, which protects all children in non-statutory daycare, ensures that pre-schools offer at least one adult to each eight children. Groups accredited by the Pre-school Learning Alliance aim to provide one:five. These high ratios benefit all children, ensuring that there is always an adult on hand, to support, observe,

1 For further information about this area of responsibility see page 31.

stimulate and question, and to join in the fun. For children with special needs this high level of adult input is especially important. It makes possible an individual approach to each child's needs and progress and allows the early detection of cause for concern as well as closely focussed monitoring of progress.

It is the high adult:child ratio in pre-schools also which makes the keyworker system such a success. Each regular worker in the pre-school has special responsibility for a few - usually five or six - children with whom a specially close relationship is established. It is the keyworker, very often, who visits the child at home before admission to the group and introduces the family to the group's systems, including its shared record-keeping. This close contact with the home and the child provides an ideal foundation for the liaison systems required by the Code of Practice.

Premises

Pre-schools must consider the suitability of their premises by assessing both facilities and access. It may be necessary to talk with owners about access to the building, toilet facilities, width of doors, room for wheelchairs and space for the storage of wheelchairs. Hall committees may be able to apply for grants for this work; making the building appropriate for people with disabilities will be an issue for other users as well as the pre-school. It may be possible for users to submit a joint grant application.

Pre-school curriculum

The pre-school leader has responsibility for planning an appropriate curriculum for all children, including those with special educational needs, and for reporting back to the committee or owner. A broad and balanced curriculum, carefully planned and properly implemented for all children, will be appropriate for most children with special educational needs. Like their peers, they learn through rich first hand experiences. The procedures used to identify the individual needs of each child and then to plan to meet those needs will apply equally for children with special educational needs. These should involve:

- carefully observing children, using a variety of observation methods to gain evidence of each child's attainment and progress

- keeping records which celebrate each child's attainments and progress

- setting objectives which will make clear the next steps in the development of the child

- drawing up play plans which set out how these next steps are to be achieved

- using the information from the play plans to fine tune individual session plans to make sure that the activities and the adult support are appropriate for the child with special educational needs

- ensuring that parents have every opportunity to be involved with the assessment of their child and with developing and implementing his/her play plan.

Development plans

The development plan will show how the pre-school plans to improve its practice including its work with children with special educational needs. Information from staff appraisals will help identify the training needed by staff, special educational needs co-ordinator, committee members and parents in order to implement the development plan. The training is likely to include information about the requirements of the Code of Practice. There may also be a need for specialised training relating to a particular aspect of special educational needs work or for general training on, for example, the identification and assessment of children's needs and the planning of the curriculum. Information about local training, including the Diploma in Pre-school Practice, Curriculum Planning Course and Special Needs Courses, is available from regional centres and local sub-committees.

Partnership with parents

Relationships between the parents and the pre-school are central to the education of every child and they are even more important for a child under five with special educational needs.
The concerns of the parent about the child may first be shared informally with the keyworker or pre-school leader. These should be listened to carefully and taken seriously. Examples of parents' worries being dismissed by professionals are all too frequent; however, pre-school staff should provide from the beginning a friendly, supportive listening ear, and they have an important continuing role to support and advise the family.

Parents should be involved in the assessment of their own child and in the development of his/her play plan. Parents may wish to be involved with their own child during pre-school sessions or they may prefer a well earned break during the sessions.

Partnership with outside agencies

Pre-schools should have information from the local education authority about local procedures for the identification of special educational needs. They should also have a list of and develop links with :

- relevant officers and professionals in the local education authority including receiving primary schools

- social services staff

- health authority personnel, including the child development centre or team

- relevant national voluntary organisations, such as Portage.

Confidentiality

Children's special needs cannot be met by one adult working in isolation and the staff will necessarily share insights and information with parents and with one another in order to support the child's development. However, the general policies on confidentiality held by most pre-schools will ensure that knowledge is shared on a 'need to know' basis.

Pre-schools can then draw on the help and advice of outside professionals as and when necessary. In particular pre-schools should be familiar with any local "moderating group" set up by the local education authority to ensure the consistent application of the criteria for statutory assessment; they may wish to serve on such groups.

Chapter 2

Assessment and provision
(Stages One, Two and Three)

The Code of Practice involves a five-stage model of

- planning provision for each child
- monitoring his/her progress
- re-planning in the light of this progress.

If a child does not respond to the programme at one stage, the next stage is triggered, and professional expertise from outside the pre-school is gradually introduced. In cases of profound and complex disability the initial stages may on occasion be by-passed after full consultation with parents, local authority and specialist advisers.

Stage One

Stage One involves the identification of a child's special educational needs by:

- gathering information about the child
- taking action to meet the child's needs within the pre-school
- monitoring and reviewing the progress made.

The trigger for Stage One is the first expression of a concern, together with evidence to substantiate this concern, often made by parents, the child's keyworker or by social services or the child health services.

If a health authority or trust, often using information from a general practitioner, considers that a child may have special educational needs, the parents and the local education authority must be informed. Parents must be provided with the names of voluntary organisations which may be of assistance, and with information about local statutory and voluntary services which might help them. These may include pre-schools, toy libraries and opportunity groups. When a child under five is referred to the local education authority by social services or the health services, agreed procedures enable the authority to decide quickly whether the child's needs require special action. The local education authority may wish to ask an educational adviser or psychologist to recommend appropriate action, such as referral for a multi-professional view at a child development centre, referral immediately for a statutory assessment (see Stage Four, page 19) , attendance at a pre-school or nursery or involvement in a home based programme such as Portage.

Once concerns have been raised in the pre-school, the keyworker will

- talk closely with the child's parents

- inform and seek advice from the pre-school's special educational needs co-ordinator

- talk to the pre-school leader

- observe the child closely and keep records in all areas of learning and development (A standard record form may be available from the local education authority; alternative proformas are included within the Pre-school Learning Alliance publication *Observation and Record Keeping* and in Appendix A.)

- with the child's parents, make an initial assessment of the child's special educational needs and set objectives which make clear the next steps to be aimed for

- draw up a play plan which sets out how these steps are to be achieved

- ensure the child continues to participate in the normal pre-school curriculum, even though the play plan may require an adjustment to the usual play activities, resources and adult roles, and to the child's teaching and/or social groups

- with the parents, monitor and review the child's progress.

A photocopiable draft Play Plan is to be found in Appendix B. Pre-schools using the plan may find it helpful to make entries in each section under two headings, distinguishing between the overall target and the specific indications by which success will be judged. For example, an entry under 'Personal & Social Development' might read as follows:

Target
Help Sarah to play near other children without disrupting them.

Success criteria
Playing alongside for increasing periods of time, without:
- biting her neighbours
- taking toys in use by other children
- knocking down other children's constructions.

The pre-school's special educational needs co-ordinator has a special role to play. He/she will ensure that the child is included on the pre-school's special educational needs register, will help the keyworker and the parents to assess the child's needs and will advise and support as necessary all the other staff in the pre-school who will have regular, routine contact with the child. Where a child is thought to have difficulties such as hearing or sight impairment, the special educational needs co-ordinator will immediately refer the child to the relevant health service.

At this stage it is important that the pre-school begins to work with parents to document full information about the child. As well as keeping records of the child's language and other areas of development, it will be important to document such things as behaviour, choice of activities and concentration span. Input will be needed from parents about the child's health, development, behaviour and interests, as well as any factors which are contributing to the special educational need. Parents' views must be taken into account with regard to any action proposed by the pre-school. The child might be able to provide a view about the things he or she finds difficult and what might help. Information may be available from outside sources, such as health or social services staff or educational psychologists.

In the light of the information gained the keyworker, parents and special educational needs coordinator will decide whether to

- continue with the current arrangements

or

- give the child special attention, further adjusting the activities and teaching methods of the pre-school

or

- seek advice and support outside the pre-school.

Throughout Stage One, keyworkers, special educational needs co-ordinators and parents should be setting dates at which to review the child's progress. Reviews will normally be held at least once a term. The review will focus on:

- the child's progress

- the degree to which the special help provided so far has been effective
- future action.

There are several possible outcomes of reviews:

- If progress is satisfactory, the child continues at Stage One. Targets continue to be set and reviewed. If progress remains satisfactory after two reviews, the time between reviews may be increased.
- If progress continues to be satisfactory, special help may no longer be needed.
- If after two review periods at Stage One, the special help provided has not enabled the child to meet the targets, the child moves to Stage Two.

Stage Two

At Stage Two the pre-school's special educational needs co-ordinator, working closely with the parents and keyworker, takes a lead in assessing the child's learning difficulty and planning, monitoring and reviewing the provision. The keyworker and other staff continue to work with the child during sessions.

Pre-school and parents continue to gather information about the child. It will be important to know whether the child is on the child protection register and whether the local authority has any responsibility for the child under the Children Act. On the basis of all the information, the special educational needs co-ordinator, working with parents and other staff, will decide whether to seek further advice and/or to draw up for the child an individual education plan. This plan, similar to the play plan recommended by the Pre-school Learning Alliance for all children, will be drawn up in close consultation with the parents and keyworker. It will build on the curriculum the child is already following and will be implemented during normal pre-school sessions. The plan will detail:

- the nature of the learning difficulties
- any pastoral care or medical needs
- the educational programme and the staff to be involved. The need for additional support from a one-to-one worker may be identified at this stage.

- input from parents
- the targets to be achieved, with timescales
- the arrangements for monitoring and assessing progress and the date for reviewing the arrangements.

The basic play plan in Appendix B may be used for this purpose, covering under each developmental heading the staff and other resources to be provided to help the child reach the targets. Providers in a local area often find it helpful if they all use the same form, either this one or one supplied by the local authority.

The special educational needs co-ordinator, the keyworker and the parents will conduct a review at Stage Two which will focus on:

- the progress made by the child at home and at the pre-school
- the effectiveness of the individual education plan
- any new information and advice
- future action.

Reviews will normally be held at least termly. The outcome of the review may be:

- The child continues at Stage Two. If progress has been at least satisfactory a new individual education plan will be drawn up setting further targets. If progress remains satisfactory after two review periods the period between reviews will be increased

or

- If the child's progress continues to be satisfactory, the child no longer needs provision under Stage Two. The child may then be recorded as having special educational needs at Stage One. If the special educational provision has been wholly successful, the child may no longer need any special help, but the child's name will be retained on the special educational needs register until it is clear that the child's progress will no longer give cause for concern.

or

- If after up to two review periods at Stage Two the special help already provided has proved insufficient to enable the child to meet the targets, additional expert advice will be sought and the child moves to Stage Three.

Stage Three

At Stage Three a different approach to meeting the child's needs is adopted; the pre-school calls upon external specialist support to help the child. The involvement of outside agencies at this stage will be new to some groups. However, this is a very positive feature of the Code and will lead to much better inter-agency working. The special educational needs co-ordinator now shares responsibility with these external services while continuing to work closely with the keyworker and parents.

Special educational needs co-ordinators should be familiar with what services are available locally. The local authority can provide information about the range of services available in their area. These are likely to include teachers of hearing and visually impaired children, language and speech therapists, physiotherapists, the educational psychology services and social services. Arrangements for securing help from these services will be affected by local policies.

On the basis of the advice from the specialist support service and from all the information gathered, the child's parents and special educational needs co-ordinator will decide whether to seek further advice from other agencies and/or to draw up a new individual education plan involving the support services. The new plan will be developed with the help of external specialists but will be implemented during normal pre-school sessions. It will describe the new strategies for supporting the child's education and will set out:

- the nature of the child's learning difficulty

- the action to be taken, the educational programme and the role of the pre-school staff

- the targets to be achieved in a given time

- the help from home

- the external specialists, including the frequency and timing of their visits and the approach to be adopted (The plan will specify for example whether specialists will work directly with the child, or indirectly, by providing advice and support to the parents, special educational needs co-ordinators, keyworkers and other staff.)

- any special activities, materials or equipment needed

- any pastoral care or medical needs

- the arrangements for monitoring and assessment and the date and arrangements for the review.

The special educational needs co-ordinator will convene Stage Three review meetings. Parents should always be invited and assisted to attend these meetings so that they fully understand and endorse the outcome, and external specialists should provide professional analysis and advice. The meeting will consider the progress made by the child, the effectiveness of the individual education plan, any future action and whether the child is likely to need a statutory assessment at Stage Four. A written record of the review meeting should be kept. The outcome of the review will be:

- The child continues at Stage Three. If the child's progress has been at least satisfactory, a new individual education plan will be drawn up setting new targets. If progress remains satisfactory after two review periods, the period between reviews is likely to be increased.

or

- The child moves to Stage One or Two. If the child's progress continues to be at least satisfactory for at least two review periods the child no longer needs external help and education under Stage Three. The child may then be recorded as having special educational needs at Stages One or Two and will receive help appropriate to that stage.

or

- If by the second Stage Three review it is clear that the child still needs more intensive support, the pre-school leader, on the advice of the special educational needs co-ordinator and in consultation with parents, will consider advising the local education authority that a statutory assessment may be necessary.

Chapter 3

Statutory assessment and statement
(Stages Four and Five)

The needs of the vast majority of children with special educational needs will be met under Stages One, Two or Three. In a minority of cases (perhaps 2% of children) it will be necessary for the local education authority to make a statutory assessment of educational needs. This statutory assessment is the focus of Stage Four. Although the local education authority takes responsibility for deciding whether to make a statutory assessment, the pre-school, working closely with parents and external specialist services, remains responsible for providing the day-to-day curriculum and support which the child needs.

Stage Four: Statutory assessment

Statutory assessment involves :

- Consideration by the local education authority, working closely with parents, the pre-school and other agencies, about whether a statutory assessment is necessary

- If so, conducting the assessment, working closely with everyone involved.

Statutory assessment will not always lead to a statement. The information gathered during an assessment may show that a child's needs can be met in the pre-school without the need for a statement. For example, it may be that a particular piece of equipment will allow the pre-school to meet the child's needs and a statement will not be necessary.

A formal request for a statutory assessment may be made to the local education authority by:

- a pre-school or other agency

or

- a parent.

Request by a pre-school or other agency

The pre-school may conclude that a statutory assessment is required because the child's needs are so substantial that they cannot be met properly within the resources normally available. This may be indicated by the child's failure to progress at Stages One, Two and Three. In a very small number of cases the pre-school may consider that statutory assessment is necessary even though there has been no special provision under Stages One, Two or Three. "Other agencies" may include health or social services departments.

Pre-schools which, after full consultation with parents, decide to request an assessment should submit full information about the child to the local education authority. This should include:

- the views of parents and, where appropriate, the views of the child on the earlier stages of assessment

- evidence from health checks

- evidence where appropriate from social services

- the written plans at Stages Two and Three

- the reviews of each individual plan

- evidence of the involvement and views of relevant outside specialist help.

Before making an assessment the local education authority must write to the parents ("serve a notice on" parents) to explain their proposal to make an assessment. It must inform parents of:

- the assessment procedures

- the name of the local authority officer who will provide further information

- parents' rights to send in evidence within a given time limit (not less than 29 days)

- sources of independent advice, eg voluntary organisations and local support groups which may help them to consider their child's needs

- the role of a "named person" who is independent of the local education authority and can give parents advice about their child's special educational needs. He/she may be for example the pre-school keyworker or special educational needs co-ordinator. The named person can attend meetings, help parents to express opinions and encourage parents to take part at all stages. The named person should be chosen in consultation with the child's parent(s).

- the full range of state, voluntary and special schools available locally so that parents can have opportunities to consider their child's future placement and arrange visits as necessary

- parents' right to request the authority to consult specialists of the parents' own choice in addition to those whom the authority is obliged to consult.

Assessment can be very stressful for parents and they need early information and support to ensure that they contribute as much as possible to the assessment of their child. Pre-school staff and other parents have an important role to play in this respect. The environment of mutual trust and support which is fostered in all good pre-schools is invaluable to parents at this time.

The local education authority proposal to make a statutory assessment must be copied to the social services department, the district health authority and the pre-school. This provides an early opportunity for the services to gather together the records which the local authority will need.

Request by a parent

The local education authority must agree to a parent's request for an assessment unless it has recently made a statutory assessment (within six months of the date of the request) or unless it concludes after looking at all the available evidence that an assessment is not necessary.

If all agencies have been working closely together at Stage Three a request from a parent for a statutory assessment should come as no surprise. But a parental request may reflect dissatisfaction or disagreement with the action taken at Stages One to Three. The local education authority should contact parents promptly to investigate further the nature of their concerns, to establish their involvement with the special educational provision already made at pre-school and to give them more details of the assessment process. It must inform the pre-school leader that parents have made a request and should ask for written evidence about the child, particularly the assessment of the child's learning difficulty and information about any special educational provision that has already been made. The local education authority should notify the educational psychology service and any other agencies, including officers of the district health authority and the social services department who may be asked for advice later.

Making the assessment and statement
The local education authority must decide whether or not to make an assessment. It should consider all the facts thoroughly, make objective judgements and reach decisions as quickly as possible. (See Appendix C for timescales prescribed by the Code of Practice.)

Criteria for deciding to make a statutory assessment
The Department for Education and Employment has set out guidance about the evidence local education authorities should seek from parents and pre-schools in deciding whether a statutory assessment should be made. The authority will look at the evidence provided by the pre-school and the parents about the nature, extent and cause of the child's learning difficulty and the action taken by the pre-school and in the home to meet and overcome the difficulties. The DfEE guidance does not set out hard and fast rules and decisions will rest on local interpretation of the guidance and local judgements about the evidence provided in each case. Some local education authorities have set up a moderating group to ensure consistency across the authority and some have worked closely with neighbouring authorities to establish agreed criteria so that some consistency exists across a number of local authorities. Evidence which local education authorities will consider includes:

- the nature of the child's learning difficulties

- the special provision which has been made for the child at Stages One, Two and Three

- the child's progress and attainment in the context of the level achieved by the child's peers

- medical conditions and health problems, which may lead to absence from pre-school and/or difficulties in concentrating or participating

- physical disabilities

- hearing or visual problems

- problems in home circumstances

- speech or language difficulties

- any emotional or behavioural difficulties

- poor attendance at pre-school.

Drawing on the evidence, the local education authority now decides whether a statutory assessment is required. If it decides not to make an assessment it must write informing the parents and the pre-school of that decision. This may be extremely disappointing to the parents and to the pre-school. The local education authority should therefore give full reasons for its decision. It should offer suggestions which will help the pre-school to meet the child's needs and if there is disagreement between the parents and the pre-school it may arrange a meeting between the two.

However, the local education authority may conclude that a statutory assessment will help the child and decide to proceed with the assessment. Parents must be informed of this decision and the reasons and should be told that their child may be called for assessment. They should know of their right to be present at any interview, test, medical examination or other assessment. They should also be given the name of a specific LEA office who will be their point of contact throughout the assessment proceedings.

In order to make a statutory assessment the local education authority will seek written advice from parents, the pre-school and the educational, medical, psychological and social services. They will also consult other sources as appropriate, such as for example the view of the child, and of Service Children's Education (SCE) for children whose parents are members of the armed forces. An important part of the assessment is likely to be observing the child during the session at pre-school. The Code sets time limits for the process of making assessments (see Appendix C).

Stage Five: Statements of special educational need

Following the receipt of all the relevant advice the local education authority must assess the child and decide whether to make a statement. In a small number of cases the local education authority will decide that a child's learning difficulties or disabilities are so severe as to require a statement of special educational need. This is because the child's needs cannot reasonably be provided within the resources normally available to the pre-school; the issuing of a statement may then involve the local education authority in making additional resources available. Most voluntary pre-schools operate against a background of severe financial hardship and urgently require additional resources to meet the needs of children with special educational needs. However, the making of a statement may not lead to additional resources being allocated directly to the pre-school, although the local education authority will be providing support as it fulfils its statutory responsibility to monitor the child's progress and review the statement through the multi-disciplinary review process.

In deciding whether to draw up a statement the local education authority must consider all the information from the statutory assessment. It will also want to confirm:

- that the assessment and the provision made by the pre-school in Stages One to Four have been appropriate
- that in spite of the provision the child has not been progressing sufficiently well
- what further provision may be needed and whether this can be made within the pre-school's resources
- whether the child's learning difficulties call for occasional support and advice from external specialists, or minor building alterations and access to particular pieces of equipment, or whether more regular and daily support, significant building modification and major pieces of equipment are needed
- the appropriateness of the child's existing placement and whether it might be helpful to move from mainstream to specialist provision.

Decision not to issue a statement
The local education authority may conclude from the assessment process that the child's special educational needs can be met from within the pre-school's own resources, with or without professional help from outside the pre-school. In this case,

a statement will be considered unnecessary. The decision not to issue a statement may be disappointing to parents and seen as a refusal to grant additional resources to their child. The local education authority should consider issuing a note in lieu of a statement, setting out the reasons for its conclusions with the supporting evidence from the statutory assessment. This evidence can be used by all those working with the child to supplement their plans for meeting the child's special educational needs. The local education authority may wish to arrange a meeting with the parents and the pre-school to discuss the decision not to statement. The LEA will also inform parents of the procedure to follow if they wish to appeal against the authority's decision by referring the matter to the Special Needs Tribunal.

The statutory assessment process ends when the local education authority decide that they will make a statement. A statement contains six parts:

Part 1 - introduction
The child's name, address, date of birth and other basic information

Part 2 - the special educational needs
What a child can and cannot do, giving details of each of the child's special educational needs as identified during the statutory assessment

Part 3 - the special educational provision
This identifies the provision the local education authority considers is necessary. The statement should provide information about:

- the objectives which the special educational provision should meet

- the provision which the local education authority considers appropriate to meet these objectives

- the arrangements for monitoring and reviewing progress.

Part 4 - the placement
This identifies the type and name of the pre-school setting where the provision specified in Part 3 will be made, or the arrangements for the education to be made away from a group or school setting. Pre-schools and nurseries may feature under Part 4. (This part is left blank in proposed statements so that the local education

authority does not pre-empt the preferences which parents may state.)

Part 5 - the non-educational needs
These must be specified and may have been identified for example by health and social services or other agencies.

Part 6 - the non-educational provision required
This is the provision required to meet the non-educational needs as specified by health and social services personnel.

The advice and information provided during the assessment stage will be appended to the statement.

The proposed statement

Initially the local education authority draws up a proposed statement completing all parts except Part 4, and sends copies to parents and to all those who have provided advice during the making of the assessment.

It is important that parents understand that they have a right to express a preference for the type of provision they wish their child to attend. For very young children access to a home based learning programme or the services of a peripatetic teacher for the hearing or visually impaired may provide the most appropriate help. Parents may wish their child, instead or in addition, to attend a pre-school or opportunity pre-school.

Although local education authorities have a duty to ensure that children with statements are educated within mainstream provision, including pre-schools as appropriate, the duty is qualified by the fact that the placement must also be:

- *appropriate* to the child's needs

- *compatible* with the interests of the other children

- *consistent* with the efficient use of the local education authority's resources.

The local education authority should inform parents that all pre-schools and nurseries in receipt of public funding under the government's nursery education scheme must publish information about their policies on special educational needs. The authority should encourage parents to visit pre-school settings and to ask to see policies and other documents to assist them to make up their minds about their child's placement.

The local education authority has a duty to name the parents' preferred pre-school in a statement providing the parents' choice is consistent with the three criteria listed above. If the local education authority does not name the parents' first choice of pre-school in a statement it must give its reasons in writing.

Every effort should be made to ensure that parents are happy with the proposed statement and that they understand the reasons for the proposals and consider that their wishes have been given proper consideration. Similar efforts should be made to ensure that, as far as possible, the child's views also are considered within the proposed statement. Local education authority staff must give parents time to discuss any anxieties about the proposed statement with the named local education authority officer and as far as possible to come to a mutual agreement.

The final statement

Once agreed the final statement should be issued immediately. (See Appendix C for the time limits set by the Code of Practice.) Local education authorities must arrange the special educational provision and any non educational provision specified in the statement. The statement should also inform parents about their options with regard to the 'named person' (See p.20). Parents who are not satisfied with the final statement may appeal to the Special Needs Tribunal, and the local authority paperwork will include information on how to go about this.

The pre-school or nursery is responsible for delivering the educational programme specified in the child's statement and as a condition of receiving a Nursery Education Grant is required to allow the local authority maintaining the statement access to the premises to monitor this provision. Nursery owners and committee members in charitable groups should have access to a child's statement in line with their duty to provide appropriately for children with special educational needs and should remember the need for confidentiality about the child in question. The special educational needs co-ordinator should also be familiar with the statement and should ensure that the child's special educational needs are made known to all those who will be working with him or her. The pre-school's special educational needs co-ordinator and the child's keyworker or one-to-one helper must monitor and review the child's progress throughout the year. Many local education authorities provide proformas and documents to assist pre-schools with this work. In some cases continuous monitoring and assessment of a child will also be the responsibility of a relevant external specialist. The child's individual educational plan will be reviewed regularly using information from parents and ensuring that parents are informed about the way they can support their child's learning at home.

Reviewing the statement

Local education authorities have the power to review statements at any time but must review them at least annually for children of school age and at least every six months for under-fives. Given the relatively short time that a child is likely to be in the pre-school, it is quite rare for pre-school staff to have to conduct a review. However, when a review is necessary its purpose is to assess the child's progress towards agreed targets. It brings together a range of views to ensure that the child is achieving the planned outcomes and if necessary the statement is modified in line with changing needs and provision. The review will :

- flag up the child's achievements as well as noting any difficulties there may be
- evaluate the special provision made for the child
- consider whether the statement continues to be appropriate and whether to cease to maintain the statement
- set new targets for the next period, if the statement is to be maintained.

The review meeting

It is the responsibility of the appointed education officer to ensure that there is an appropriate review of the child's statement of special educational needs.

At least two months before the review date, the appointed education officer will write to the pre-school leader with a copy to the child's parents, asking the leader to convene the meeting and to prepare the necessary reports. The pre-school leader is responsible for arranging the meeting, organising reports and sending them to the local education authority. At least six weeks before the meeting the leader invites a representative of the local education authority, other relevant specialists and parents to attend the meeting and to provide written reports. Parents should be encouraged to write down their views about the child's progress, to attend the meeting and to take an active part in deciding about the new targets. At least two weeks before the meeting the pre-school leader will send copies of all reports to those invited to attend.

The meeting normally takes place within the pre-school and should be chaired by the pre-school leader or another member of staff. After the meeting the pre-school leader completes a review form summarising the outcomes of the meeting and setting out new targets. This form is sent to all those concerned with the review, including the local education officer, parents and other relevant specialists. The education officer reviews the statement in the light of this new information and makes recommendations. These are circulated to all concerned with the review.

Assessment of children under two

Children under two with special educational needs may attend day nurseries in membership of the Pre-school Learning Alliance and may attend parent and toddler pre-schools along with their parents.

When a child under two is referred to the local education authority it is likely that any special needs will have been identified by the child's parents, the child health services or social services. The child is likely to have a particular condition or major health problem which has caused concern at a very early age. Assessment of children under two need not follow the statutory procedures which apply to children of two and over.

It is rare for children under two to have a statement of special educational needs and the procedures for making such a statement are not specified in legislation. The local authority may prefer to make voluntary agreements to cover the arrangements for the child but they should be aware that a request from a parent for statutory assessment could indicate dissatisfaction with the arrangements which have been made. For very young children local education authorities will consider home based programmes such as Portage or peripatetic services for children with hearing or visual impairments. Parents should be consulted about the help and support they would like to receive. Some may prefer to attend a child development centre or to combine home-based with centre-based support.

If a child has very complex needs or needs access to a particular programme of home based teaching or developmental play, a decision may be made to issue a statement. The statement will include:

- all available information about the child, with clear details of the special educational needs

- a record of the views of parents and relevant professionals

- a clear description of the services being offered, including the contribution of the education services and of any other statutory or voluntary agencies

- the arrangements for monitoring and reviewing a statement.

It is important to monitor the child's progress carefully. Local education authorities will work in partnership with service providers to collect that information which can identify and meet children's special educational needs. This can avoid duplication of investigations when the child is over two.

Chapter **4**

Staffing in pre-schools

Implementing the Code of Practice can have a very favourable impact on staff and volunteers in pre-schools:

- The need to allocate new responsibilities can result in a more satisfying definition of roles within the pre-school.

- The challenge of new ways of working can generate fresh learning and enthusiasm.

- The creation of new roles offers opportunities for personal and professional development to a greater number of staff and volunteer members. People with a particular interest in special needs work might choose to become involved on a one:one basis with a child who needs a high level of support. The post of special educational needs co-ordinator also creates in the pre-school an additional senior role . This may involve producing reports for the pre-school leader, the committee/owner and possibly for the local authority, as well as using and developing administrative, management and other skills within the pre-school.

The special educational needs co-ordinator

The DfEE Code of Practice on the Identification and Assessment of Special Educational Needs requires that one member of staff take on the role of special educational needs co-ordinator. This person carries overall responsibility, not necessarily for day to day interaction with children with special needs, but for making sure that the pre-school's special needs policy is put into practice. In particular, the special educational needs co-ordinator will:

Be familiar with the requirements of the Code of Practice
At least one person in the pre-school should become really familiar with the Code of Practice. Not only does the Code make clear the obligations of the pre-school with regard to children with special educational needs, but it also indicates sources of support for the work, especially in the form of links with the local authority staff and services.

Maintain a central register of children with special educational needs
Personal details on the development of individual children may be confidential and will be kept in their own files, but the special educational needs co-ordinator will maintain a general register of children with special educational needs.

Ensure that records are kept on children with special educational needs
Routine observations and record keeping together with action plans for children with special educational needs will include details of the educational need as observed/assessed and the steps taken to meet the child's special need(s).

Ensure that there is close liaison with parents of children with special educational needs
The special educational needs co-ordinator will not necessarily in person be in contact with all parents of children with special educational needs; this role may more properly be in the hands of the child's keyworker. However, the special educational needs co-ordinator is responsible for ensuring that systems are in place to keep parents fully informed and to act on parents' insights and information into the needs and development of their own children.

Provide a link between the pre-school and external services
These services will include relevant voluntary organisations, educational psychologists, child and family guidance centres, therapists, medical services and Alliance development workers.

Disseminate information
The special educational needs co-ordinator will ensure that relevant information is shared with other staff and with parents, and will support the training and professional development of other staff members involved in working with children with special educational needs.

The role of the special educational needs co-ordinator is therefore an important one and the pre-school committee/owner should give careful thought to who should do it.

- In some pre-schools the pre-school leader will be the appropriate person. The leader is already responsible for co-ordinating the work of the pre-school on a day to day basis, so it is possible that special needs work may be a natural extension of this responsibility.

- Where the pre-school leader is already over-burdened with administration and other duties, it might be more sensible to make the work of the special educational needs co-ordinator part of the role of a deputy/assistant pre-school leader.

- Sometimes there is another member of staff ready and willing to progress in knowledge and responsibility and such a person might welcome the challenge of taking on the role of special educational needs co-ordinator. This has the advantage of spreading more widely the opportunities for personal and professional development within the group.

In some large groups, the special educational needs co-ordinator may head a team of people.

Whoever takes on the role of special educational needs co-ordinator will need to work closely with the key workers of children with special educational needs. It may sometimes be appropriate for a co-ordinator plus relevant key workers together to form the special educational needs co-ordinating team. There are implications for in-service training for workers who wish to progress in this area.

One-to-one workers

Not all children with special educational needs will require an additional one-to-one worker. However, the presence of a supernumerary one-to-one worker can enable some children with special needs to participate fully in the pre-school session, deriving maximum pleasure and benefit from being there. Children with a physical handicap or who suffer from a visiual or hearing impairment are among those who can benefit from the help of a one-to-one worker. For this reason, many pre-schools fundraise specifically to provide one-to-one workers where necessary. They may be either volunteer or staff members of the pre-school. Sometimes adults who are developing a particular interest in special needs welcome the opportunity to work closely with a particular child.

Some pre-schools fundraise to support these posts, or seek grant aid to ensure that they can employ a one-to-one worker when necessary.

The presence of a one-to-one helper ensures that a child who needs individual support can have it without depriving other children in the group of the high adult:child ratio which all young children need. However, children with special educational needs, like all other children, need opportunities to establish their own areas of independence and to make relationships with an expanding range of adults. The one-to-one helper may not therefore overtly 'shadow' the child for whom s/he has a special responsibility, as this might risk limiting the child's development. What the helper will do is :

- Work closely with the child's keyworker in building up a body of knowledge and understanding about the child's attainments, potential, interests and developmental stage

- Develop a relationship with the child

- Deal as necessary with the child's personal needs (This makes it especially important for the helper to be a familiar person who works regularly with the child.)

- Observe the child during the pre-school session, ensuring that s/he is happy, comfortable and engaged in appropriate activities

- Be responsible for making sure that the child's activities and interactions in the group contribute to her/his individual play plan

- Create and co-ordinate individual records, in liaison with the keyworker, on the child's development and progress, in co-operation with the special educational needs co-ordinator

- Maintain close contact with the child's parents to ensure that parents and pre-school can work together for the child's interests, sharing aims and insights

- Maintain a close, though discreet, watch on the child's physical safety and well-being as necessary.

Other staff and helpers

A child with special educational needs is not the responsibility only of her/his one-to-one helper, keyworker and/or special needs co-ordinator. Children with special needs enter the group on the same terms as all other children. Like other children they will be part of a keyworker group. Like other children they have an agreed play plan and all the adults present will pull together to ensure on a day-to-day basis that the play plans are implemented and that the curriculum of the group as a whole meets the needs of the individual children within it, including those who have special needs of any kind.

All the adults are responsible, likewise, for ensuring that other children in the group are helped positively to respect and respond to one another in ways which are free of stereotypical expectations about children and adults with special educational needs, or about any other group.

Training

Training for the support of children with special educational needs is available through the Pre-school Learning Alliance and people interested in extending their skills and knowledge in this way should contact their regional centre for advice about the nearest available course.

Under the Code of Practice, all agencies, both voluntary and statutory, should work together to support children with special educational needs. Pre-schools should find out from the local education authority whether there is in-service training for their own staff which pre-school personnel could share.

In some cases, the special educational needs co-ordinator will be the person to attend any available training. However, if the whole pre-school is to fulfil its responsibilities to children with special educational needs and their families, training should not be focused on just one person. All members of the pre-school - staff, leader(s), special needs co-ordinator, parents and committee/owner - need opportunities to learn more. If the special educational needs co-ordinator is the person who attends a course - and sometimes limitations on funding may make this inevitable - there should be a structure in place to ensure that the special educational needs co-ordinator has a duty and the opportunity to pass on new ideas and information.

Not all training takes the form of a course. Parents and staff should also be enabled and encouraged to attend:

- Conferences/workshops led by speakers with specific expertise
- Training events organised by other organisations, especially other charities dealing with specific learning difficulties
- Informal opportunities to exchange ideas and experiences with people from other pre-schools, perhaps at lunchtime meetings organised by the local Alliance sub-committee
- Branch/county sub-committee open meetings. These can be a useful way of spreading the cost of obtaining good speakers. If there is widespread concern in the area about, for example, children with speech and language problems, a good speaker at a well advertised evening or Saturday morning meeting will attract a large audience. A small charge to non-members will help defray costs.

Whatever form of training is made available, the pre-school needs systems to ensure that the new learning spreads throughout the group rather than remaining concentrated in one or two people. Systems for sharing knowledge might include:

- Written reports posted on the noticeboard and/or circulated at staff/committee meetings
- Brief spoken feedback either at staff meetings or at the end of the day/session just after the children have gone home
- 'Cascaded' learning sessions, where one or two people who have received training pass on the new information and advice to others
- Encouraging all those who attend training to bring away any useful handouts and to circulate these in the group.

Chapter **5**

Record keeping

The record keeping system already available to pre-schools has the capacity to meet most of the requirements of the Code of Practice. The formative record sheets and action plan forms in the Pre-school Learning Alliance *Observation & Record keeping* book provide opportunities to:

- Receive input from parents

- Create a dated chronological record

- Devise plans specific to the needs of each child

- Record the child's progress in particular areas of learning and development once the plans are put into effect.

Pre-school Learning Alliance records are especially valuable for use with children with special educational needs because of their 'can do' approach. They emphasise the positive aspects of children's learning and development, identifying achievements, however small, rather than listing failures.

In addition, for a child who has or might have special educational needs, a dated record should be kept of:

- The initial cause for concern

- The source of this information (parent, doctor, pre-school worker, social worker)

- The first discussions with parent(s) about the child's possible special educational need

- The views of parents and of any other person(s) with a relevant input to make

- The steps taken at all stages of the Code of Practice to meet the child's special educational need, including the role of the adults, equipment/activities, targets set and date for review. The adults involved will include parents and, at Stage Three, outside agencies as appropriate.

- Progress achieved

- Advice from relevant professionals at any stage.

This part of the child's record can be used as necessary:

- To seek outside help at Stage Three
- To initiate or contribute to the statementing process
- To pass on information to other institutions the child may attend.

A proforma which can be copied and used for this purpose can be found in Appendix A. Some local authorities have printed proformas of their own and it may sometimes be more convenient for all providers in a particular area to use the same forms. This can make a useful item for discussion at meetings of any local under-fives forum.

Reviews

Sound record keeping makes a good basis for assessing children's progress and evaluating the effectiveness of action plans.

The 'cycle of quality' identified in *Observation & Record keeping* is the right of all children, not just those with special educational needs. For any child, judgements of need must be based upon close observation. Decisions about need will then inform the nature of the provision and any changes necessary. Changes in provision will be followed by further observation.

In the case of a child with special educational needs, more specific targets may be set, together with a date for review, to ensure that the child's progress is closely monitored. As with any other child, however, evaluation of the success or otherwise of adult provision/intervention can be made only on the basis of further observation of the child in the pre-school, together with reports from parents where appropriate of the child's progress at home.

In the light of information gathered since the last review took place and/or targets were set, the following decisions may be made:

- To continue with the present course of action, targeting further progress for review at a specific time

- To amend provision in the light of observations of the child in a renewed attempt to meet targets already set

- To move to a further step in the assessment process

- To conclude that the child's assessed need has been met for now and to set a date for further review to confirm this.

Chapter 6
Links with outside agencies

Any organisation offering support for children and families with special needs must be able to draw on a wide range of resources in the local community in order to ensure that:

- When a special educational need is first suspected, immediate help is available as necessary to confirm the suspicion as appropriate and to ensure that the child receives maximum support at an early stage, which might prevent the development of additional special needs

- All aspects of the child's needs are fully addressed, drawing on a range of services as necessary

- There is continuity between the different provisions which the child may attend over a period of time.

Outside services can be an invaluable source of assistance to the pre-school, offering as appropriate:

- Information on local assessment procedures

- Practical advice on making provision in the early stages

- Sources of specialist equipment

- Access to peer support through under-fives forums and other collaborative enterprises locally

- Opportunities to join together for training purposes with staff from other sectors

- Support where necessary in accessing translation services in preparing materials for parents

- Access to local services such as specialist staff, educational psychologists and information technology support.

In order to ensure that these resources are available when needed, the pre-school should take active steps to build up contacts and resources so that when they are approached by a family with a child with special educational needs, they will have systems already in place to support both the child and the family and to access any help which may be required.

The pre-school, through its special educational needs co-ordinator, should aim to build up:

- Specific named contacts with personnel in the local education authority, social services department and health services, especially the local health visitor

- A list of contact addresses and telephone numbers for organisations specialising in the needs arising from specific disabilities and learning difficulties. In many cases there will be a national address and telephone number plus a local contact.

- Contacts with non-statutory organisations supporting the parents of children with special educational needs, such as Portage* .

The pre-school should play an active part in the local under-fives forum or any other collaborative group which draws together early years practitioners from the statutory, voluntary and private sectors. Such groups can be a useful source of shared information and expertise, in addition to a means of ensuring continuity and consistency of approach across all sectors. This consistency can help avoid confusion for the parents of children with special educational needs, who may well be involved with providers from more than one sector.

The special educational needs record on specific children initiated and held in the pre-school can be a valuable means of helping other providers to recognise what has been accomplished so far. This avoids the need for parents to explain the situation repeatedly and enables all providers to target their resources to the best advantage of the child.

* For the address of the National Portage Society and other support organisations, see page 57.

References and further reading

1   DfEE Code of Practice on the Identification and Assessment of Special Educational Needs

2. DfEE Guidance on the application of the Code to institutions outside the main sector of education

3. DfEE Special Educational Needs - a guide for parents

4. Oxfordshire Education Service - Oxfordshire stages of assessment - a handbook for pre-school provision

5. Pre-school Learning Alliance - *Pre-school Prospectus*

6. Pre-school Learning Alliance - *Observation and Record Keeping*

Appendix A

Record of individual development

This summative record shows the child's attainments in all areas of learning and development on the date indicated.

Child's name..

Pre-school setting ....

Date..

Creative/aesthetic (SCAA "Creative development")
Includes:

- responding to music, stories and visual arts/crafts

- joining in music, story-making, role play

- representing experiences using a range of media

- exploring tools and techniques to create an individual response.

Emotional development (SCAA "Personal & social development")
Includes:

- expressing feelings in acceptable ways
- recognising their own feelings in other people and in stories
- growing in self-repect and self-confidence
- extending concentration and perseverance
- developing positive attitudes to learning.

Language and literacy (SCAA "Language and literacy")
Includes:

- using language to communicate with other children and with adults
- developing an expanding vocabulary with increasingly complex sentences
- understanding the uses of written language
- using and enjoying books
- recognising some written words, including own name
- behaving as an emergent writer
- knowing and enjoying rhymes.

Mathematics (SCAA "Mathematics" and also some aspects of "Knowledge and understanding of the world")
Includes:

- identifying and manipulating shapes
- recognising and creating patterns and sequences
- developing concepts of time and space
- sorting and matching
- using a mathematical vocabulary, with words and phrases such as *more, longer, how many* and *how much*, as well as names of shapes and of mathematical processes such as adding and taking away
- counting, weighing and measuring
- beginning to understand ideas of conservation.

Moral and spiritual experience (SCAA "Personal and social development")
Includes:

- learning to behave with kindness and consideration
- becoming aware of and taking part in religious and cultural traditions - family ones and other people's
- experiencing awe and wonder
- respecting and valuing other children and adults
- showing care and compassion towards all living things.

Moving towards independence (SCAA "Personal and social development")
Includes:

- parting from parents/carers
- tackling new experiences
- practising self-maintenance skills such as dressing and toileting
- choosing, planning and reflecting on their own play projects
- accepting responsibility
- taking the lead sometimes.

Physical development (SCAA "Physical development")
Includes:

- enjoying energetic play and physical challenges
- developing stamina and fitness
- becoming increasingly skillful in using small muscles
- gaining strength and control in large muscles
- moving confidently
- climbing, running, balancing.

Science (SCAA "Knowledge and understanding of the world")
Includes:

- observing and exploring the world, including living and growing things, using their senses
- reaching conclusions based on observation and discussion
- recognising and discussing similarities and differences between things and between groups of things
- gathering information - from observation, by asking questions and through books
- seeking explanations
- making predictions, and testing them.

Social and human development (SCAA "Personal and social development" and also with some aspects of "Knowledge and understanding of the world")
Includes:

- making friends

- working as part of large and small groups

- accepting support and instruction from adults in the group

- respecting and valuing one another

- accepting and working to the rules of the group

- contributing to the life of the group

- becoming aware of the life of the local community and of changes and developments within it.

Technology (SCAA "Knowledge and understanding of the world")
Includes:

- finding out how things work

- tackling problems

- selecting and using tools

- using equipment for specific purposes, such as syphons, magnifying glasses

- using IT resources, such as programmable toys, computers, tape recorders and slide projectors.

Signature of keyworker...

Signature of pre-school leader ....

Appendix B

Play and learning plan for _____ **term** _____ **(date)**

This plan outlines the targets we shall be working towards over the next term and the outcomes on which we shall be concentrating when working and playing with:

Child's name ....

Creative/aesthetic development (SCAA "Creative development")

....

Emotional development (SCAA "Personal and social development")

....

Language and literacy (SCAA "Language and literacy")

....

Mathematics (SCAA "Mathematics" and "Knowledge and understanding of the world")

....

Moral and spiritual development (SCAA "Pesonal and social development")

....

Moving towards independence (SCAA "Personal and social development")

....

Physical development (SCAA "Physical development")

....

Science (SCAA "Knowledge and understanding of the world")

....

Social and human development (SCAA "Personal and social development" and "Knowledge and understanding of the world")

....

Technology (SCAA "Knowledge and understanding of the world")

....

These plans will be implemented on a day-to-day basis with the help of short-term plans which will indicate in more detail the resources to be provided, the size of group and the nature of the adults' input.

To be reviewed by ....

Signature of keyworker ....

Signature of pe-school leader ....

Date ....

Appendix C

Timescales for statutory assessments and statements

Time limits normally govern each step in the process of making assessments and statements.

Considering whether a statutory assessment is necessary

The period from the issue of a notice to parents informing them that they propose to make an assessment, or the receipt of a request for a statutory assessment from parents, to the decision as to whether to make a statutory assessment must normally be no more than 6 weeks.

Making the assessment

The period from the local education authority's decision to make a statutory assessment to the local education authority's decision as to whether to make a statement must normally be no more than 10 weeks.

Drafting the proposed statement or note in lieu

The period from the local education authority's decision whether to make a statement to the issue of a proposed statement, or of a notice of the local education authority's decision not to make a statement, giving full reasons, must normally be no more than 2 weeks.

Finalising the statement

The period from the issue of the proposed statement to the issue of the final copy of the statement must normally be no more than 8 weeks.

Total: 26 weeks

Appendix D
Sources of help

Action for Sick Children, Argyle House, 29-31 Euston Road, London NW1 2SD. Tel 0171 833 2041.

ADD/ADHD Support Group, 44 Drynham Road, Trowbridge, Wilts BA14 0PE.

Advisory Centre for Education (ACE), 1B Aberdeen Studios, 22 Highbury Grove London N5 2DQ. Tel 0171 354 8321.

Arthritis Care, 18 Stephenson Way, London NW1 2HD. Tel 0171 916 1500.

Association For All Speech Impaired Children, 347 Central Market, Smithfield, London EC1A 9NH. Tel 0171 236 3632/6487.

Association for Brain Damaged Children, 68 Brookside Avenue, Whobley, Coventry CV5 8AF. Tel 01203 711888.

Association for Spina Bifida and Hydrocephalus, ASBAH House, 42 Park Road, Peterborough PE1 2UQ. Tel 01733 555988.

British Diabetic Association, 10 Queen Anne Street, London W1M 0BD. Tel 0171 323 1531.

British Dyslexia Association, 98 London Road, Reading RG1 5AU. Tel 01734 668271.

British Epilepsy Association, Anstey House, 40 Hanover Square, Leeds LS3 1BE. Tel 0113 243 9393.

British Institute for Learning Disability, Wolverhampton Road, Kiddeminster DY10 3PP. Tel 01562 850251

Brittle Bone Society, 30 Guthrie Street, Dundee DD1 5BS. Tel 01382 204446.

Centre for Studies on Inclusive Education, 1 Redland Close, Elm Lane, Redland, Bristol BS6 6UE. Tel 0117 923 8450

Contact a Family 170 Tottenham Court Road, London W1P 0HA. Tel 0171 383 3555.

Council for Disabled Children, 8 Wakley Street, London EC1V 7QE. Tel 0171 843 6000.

Cystic Fibrosis Research Trust, Alexandra House, 5 Blythe Road, Bromley, Kent BR1 3RS. Tel 0181 464 7211.

Dial UK - The Disability Helpline (Nationwide telephone information and advice services) Park Lodge, St Catherine's Hospital, Tickhill Road, Bably, Doncaster DN4 8QN. Tel 01302 310123.

Disability Alliance, ERA (Publish Disability Rights Handbook) Universal House, 88-94 Wentworth Street, London E1 7SA. Tel 0171 247 8776.

Disabled Living Foundation, 380-384 Harrow Road, London W9 2HU. Tel 0171 289 6111.

Downs Syndrome Association, 155 Mitcham Road, London SW17 9PG. Tel 0181 682 4001.

Dyslexia Institute, 133 Gresham Road, Staines, Middx TW18 2AJ. Tel 01784 463851.

Family Fund Trust, PO Box 50 York YO1 2ZX. Tel 01904 621115.

Foundation for the Study of Infant Deaths, 14 Halkin Street, London SW1X 7DP. Tel 0171 235 1721.

Friedreich's Ataxia Group, The Stable, Wiggins Yard, Bridge Street, Godalming, Surrey GU7 1HW. Tel 01483 417111.

Greater London Association for Disabled People (GLAD), 336 Brixton Road, London SW9 7AA. Tel 0171 346 5800.

Haemophilia Society, 3rd Floor, Chesterfield House, 385 Euston Road, London NW1 3AU. Tel 0171 380 0600.

HAPA (formerly Handicapped Adventure Playgroup Association), Pryor's Bank, Bishops Park, London SW6 3LA. Tel 0171 736 4443.

Home-Start UK, 2 Salisbury Road, Leicester LE1 7QR. Tel 0116 233 9955.

Huntington's Disease Association, 108 Battersea High Street, London SW11 3HP. Tel 0171 223 7000.

Hyperactive Children's Support Group, 71 Whyke Lane, Chichester, Sussex PO19 2LD. Tel 01903 725182.

In Touch (For information and contacts on rare handicapped conditions), 10 Norman Road, Sale, Cheshire M33 3DF. Tel 0161 905 2440.

I CAN: Invalid Children's Aid Nationwide Barbican Citygate, 13 Dufferin Street, London EC1Y 8NA.

Lady Hoare Trust for Physically Disabled Children, 87 Worship Street, London EC2A 2BE. Tel 0171 377 7567.

Leukaemia Care Society, PO Box 82, Exeter, Devon EX2 5DP. Tel 01392 464848.

MENCAP (Royal Society for Mentally Handicapped Children and Adults), 117-123 Golden Lane, London EC1Y 0RF. Tel 0171 454 0454.

MIND (National Association for Mental Health), 15-19 Broadway, London E15 4BQ. Tel 0181 519 2122.

Motability, Goodman House, Station Approach, Harlow, Essex CM20 2ET. Tel 01279 635999.

Muscular Dystrophy Group of Great Britain 7-11 Prescott Place, London SW4 6BS. Tel 0171 720 8055.

National Autistic Society, 393 City Road, London WC1V 1NE. Tel 0171 833 2299.

National Association of Hospital Play Staff
40 High Street, Landbeach, Cambridge
CB4 4DT.

National Association of Toy and Leisure
Libraries (Play Matters), 68 Churchway,
London NW1 1LT.
Tel 0171 387 9592.

National Deaf Children's Society,
15 Dufferin Street, London EC1Y 8PD.
Tel 0171 490 8656.

National Eczema Society, 163 Eversholt
Street, London NW1 1BU.
Tel 0171 388 4097.

National Portage Association, 127 Monks
Dale, Yeovil, Somerset BA21 3JE.
Tel 01935 471641.

Network, 81 1-7 Woodfield Terrace,
Stansted, Essex CM24 8AJ.
Tel 01279 647415.

Parents for Inclusion, Unit 3, 70 South
Lambeth Road, London SW8 1RL.
Tel 0171 735 7735.

PHAB England (Physically Disabled and
Able Bodied), Summit House, Wandle
Road, Croydon, Surrey CRO 1DF.
Tel 0181 667 9443.

PLANET (Play Leisure Advice Network)
Save the Children, Cambridge House,
London W6 0LE.
Tel 0181 741 4054

REACH (National Resource Centre for
Children with Reading Difficulties),
Wellington House, Wellington Street,
Wokingham RG11 2AG.
Tel 01734 891101

Royal Association for Disability &
Rehabilitiation (RADAR), 12 City Forum,
250 City Road, London EC1V 8AF.
Tel 0171 250 3222.

Royal National Institute for the Blind,
224 Great Portland Street, London W1N
6AA. Tel 0171 388 1266.

Royal National Institute for Deaf People,
19-23 Featherstone Street, London EC1Y
8SL. 0171 296 8000.

SCOPE (formerly Spastics Society),
12 Park Crescent, London W1N 4EQ.
Tel 0171 636 5020

SENSE - The National Deafblind & Rubella
Association, 11-13 Clifton Terrace,
Finsbury Park, London N4 3SR.
Tel 0171 272 7774.

Sickle Cell Society, 54 Station Road,
London NW10 4UA. Tel 0181 961 7795.

Spinal Injuries Association, 76 St James
Lane, London N10 3DF.
Tel 0181 444 2121.

Tuberous Sclerosis Association,
Little Barnsley Farm, Catshill, Bromsgrove,
Worcs B61 0NQ. Tel 01527 871898.

Other Pre-school Learning Alliance publications

Guidelines

Good practice for sessional pre-schools
Good practice for parent and toddler pre-schools
Good practice for full and extended daycare pre-schools

Play Activities

Glueing
Make believe play
Sand and water
Clay and dough
Wood play
Books and stories

Learn Through Play

Maths through play
Science through play
Technology through play
Shapes and colours through play
Music through play
Language through play

Pre-school prospectus

Observation and record-keeping

Behaviour in pre-school

Business Side

Pre-schools as employers
Pre-school committees and constitutions

A complete list of Pre-school Learning Alliance publications and teaching resources is available for SAE from: Pre-school Learning Alliance, 69 Kings Cross Road, London WC1X 9LL.